THE
BIBLE

Storybook

THE
BIBLE

Storybook

Ten Tales From the Old and New Testaments
retold by Georgie Adams *pictures by* Peter Utton

Dial Books for Young Readers
New York

For Judith Elliott who inspired this book,

with grateful thanks and appreciation for her

invaluable editorial guidance—G.A.

To Harry—P.U.

First published in the United States 1995
by Dial Books for Young Readers
A Division of Penguin Books USA Inc.
375 Hudson Street
New York, New York 10014

Published in Great Britain 1994 by Orion Children's Books
A Division of the Orion Publishing Group Ltd.

Text copyright © 1994 by Georgie Adams
Pictures copyright © 1994 by Peter Utton
Designed by Ian Butterworth
All rights reserved
Printed in Italy
First Edition
1 3 5 7 9 10 8 6 4 2
Library of Congress Cataloging in Publication Data
Adams, Georgie.
The Bible storybook: ten tales from the Old and New Testaments
retold by Georgie Adams; pictures by Peter Utton.
p. cm.
ISBN 0-8037-1760-1
1. Bible stories, English. [1. Bible stories.] I. Utton, Peter, ill. II. Title.
BS551.2.A325 1995
220.9'505—dc20 93-40682 CIP AC

Contents

Foreword 8

Noah's Ark 10

Joseph and His Coat of Many Colors 22

Moses in the Bulrushes 32

David and Goliath 38

Daniel in the Lions' Den 48

Jonah and the Whale 56

The First Christmas 64

The Good Samaritan 72

Jesus Heals Jairus's Daughter 78

The Story of the Loaves and Fishes 84

Foreword

When I sat down to write this book, I imagined telling these stories to my children, adding my own thoughts here and there, with a good measure of humor too. Storytelling has always been a special time we spend together. With this in mind I wrote these stories to be shared orally—just as they were for hundreds and hundreds of years in tales, songs, and legends before they were actually written down and put together in the Bible.

The Bible is like a library—the word *bible* means "books." There are sixty-six smaller books that make up the one big book called the Bible. It took centuries to collect the stories and writings that make up the Bible and it would take ages to read the Bible all at once!

There are two main parts to the Bible—the Old Testament and the New Testament. The Old Testament consists of stories about God and his chosen people, the Israelites. That's where you'll find exciting stories about Noah, Joseph, and David, among others, who loved God and tried to be good. The New Testament tells about the life of Jesus, the Son of God. In this part there are stories about Jesus performing miracles and healing the sick—each one full of mystery and meaning.

But the language of the Bible is not always easy to understand. So I have chosen some of the best-loved stories and retold them. I pictured how things might have been (the Bible doesn't always say), and introduced my own ideas where I think they help to bring characters and events to life—careful always to preserve the spirit and message of these wonderful stories.

I hope you'll enjoy *The Bible Storybook* at bedtime or anytime—over and over again!

Georgie Adams

Noah's Ark

There was once a man called Noah, who loved God and tried to be good. Noah had a wife and three sons called Shem, Ham, and Japheth. Noah, his wife, the sons, and their wives all worked hard.

God was pleased with Noah and his family, but he wasn't too happy about everyone else. He looked around and saw people fighting, stealing, and telling lies. No wonder he wasn't pleased.

I'm sorry I made people, thought God. I'll destroy everything and begin again. But it didn't seem fair that Noah's family should be punished too, so God thought of a plan to save them.

"I'm going to send a flood that will drown all the wicked people and the whole earth," God told Noah one day. "But if you do as I say, you and your family will be safe."

God told Noah to build an ark. He gave him the exact measurements for the boat. It would have three decks, a window, and a door. Noah wrote the plans down carefully. The ark was going to be enormous! God explained why:

"Many animals will be lost in the flood," he said. "I want you to take a male and female of every kind on board with you. Look after them until the flood goes down. Then let them go to make new homes for their young. Remember to pack enough food for everyone."

Noah started work on the ark immediately. Shem, Ham, and

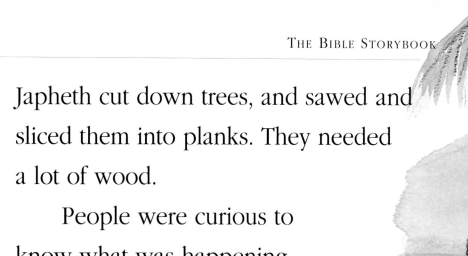

Japheth cut down trees, and sawed and sliced them into planks. They needed a lot of wood.

People were curious to know what was happening.

"There's going to be a flood," Noah told them all. "Everything and everyone will be destroyed."

Well, no one believed him for a minute. It had never rained that way before. So people laughed at Noah and went away.

While Noah was busy building the ark, his sons went to look for the animals. They rounded them up and brought them back in pairs. The animals came roaring, bleating, grunting, and squawking. What a noise!

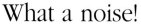

The women made a list of things they would need:

Food for the family—
fish,
bread,
rice,
melons,
dates, and figs.
Food for the animals.
Water to drink,
pots and pans . . .

It was a long list.

Meanwhile Noah put the finishing touches to the ark. He painted it with sticky tar to keep the water out. And when that was done, the ark was ready.

God told Noah that the flood would start in a week. It would rain for forty days and forty nights.

So Noah said to Shem, Ham, and Japheth, "Start loading up!"

After seven days everything was on board. As Noah watched the last two animals trot inside, he felt the first drop of rain on his head. Then he took his family into the ark, and God shut the door.

It poured. Rain fell from the sky like a sheet of water. Rivers overflowed. Fields became lakes. Lakes turned into seas.

The ark creaked and rolled, but it stayed afloat. The flood rose

higher and higher. Over the trees. Over the hills. Over the mountains!
Noah listened to the rain hammering on the roof. He could hear the
waves slapping against the hull. And still it kept raining.

One morning about six weeks later, Noah woke up and listened. He couldn't hear a thing. The rain had stopped. He looked out the window.

The sun was shining. There wasn't a cloud in sight.

It took ages for the floodwaters to go down. The ark drifted for weeks, until one day *bump!* it ran aground.

Noah opened the window and looked over the side. They seemed to be stuck on a mountain.

Everyone wanted to get out and stretch their legs, but the ark was still surrounded by water.

Noah brought a dove to the window and let it fly out.
He wanted to see if the bird could find dry land.
But the dove came back before sunset, tired and
hungry. It had found nothing.

A week later Noah sent the dove out
again. This time it came back with an olive
twig. It had found a tree to perch on.

Seven days after that, Noah sent the dove off a third time. But this time it didn't return, so he knew it had found land.

Noah opened the door. There wasn't a puddle in sight!

"Look!" cried Noah. "The flood is gone."

It was wonderful to be outside again. The world looked fresh and green after all that rain.

Noah and his family helped the animals out of the ark. They came clattering down the ramp two by two. A male and female of every kind. Every creature free to make a new start.

God promised Noah that he would never send another flood to destroy the world. And when God makes a promise, he keeps it.

"I'll give you a sign," said God. "Whenever it's cloudy and a rainbow appears in the sky, you will know that I have remembered my promise to you, your family, and all the animals. No more floods!"

God kept his word, and little by little news about the rainbow spread around the world.

Joseph
and His Coat of Many Colors

There was a boy called Joseph who had eleven brothers. It was a job keeping everyone happy in that family, I can tell you. Once, Joseph told his father that his older brothers were neglecting the flocks. It made them angry with Joseph.

Jacob, the boys' father, loved Joseph more than all the rest, which wasn't fair, but that's how it was. One day he gave his favorite son a fine coat of many colors. There wasn't another one like it for miles around. And Joseph wore it everywhere.

All this made his brothers very jealous.

"Look at us," said Judah. "Here we are watching the animals and cutting corn. And what's Joseph doing? Wandering around in that new coat, daydreaming!"

It was true. Joseph was a dreamer. At night he had strange dreams that he could remember clearly the next day.

"Listen to this," Joseph said to his brothers one morning. "In my dream we were bundling corn into sheaves. Suddenly my sheaf stood up straight and your sheaves bowed down to it."

Joseph's brothers didn't like the sound of that.

"How dare you suggest that we should bow to you!" said Daniel.

It was only a dream, but that's what it meant. It made the brothers even angrier.

A few days later Joseph had another dream. This time he told the whole family about it.

"In my dream I saw the sun, the
moon, and eleven stars all bow
down to me," said Joseph.

Well, that did it. Even his father was angry. The sun and moon
sounded very much like Jacob and his wife. You can guess who the
eleven stars were!

Although he was upset, Jacob thought a lot about
this dream. Could it be a sign from God that Joseph
was to be the most special person in the family?

There came a time when the family's sheep and
goats had eaten everything except a few scrubby

bushes. So one day the brothers—all except Joseph and little Benjamin—packed their lunches and took the animals to better land.

After a while Jacob began to worry. He asked Joseph to go and look for them.

"Make sure they are safe," said Jacob, as he waved good-bye to his favorite son.

It took Joseph a long time to find his brothers. Up one hill and down another. It was exhausting. And, of course, he insisted on wearing that coat! But at last he saw them.

Perhaps the sight of that coat brought all the feelings of jealousy back to them, because at that moment his brothers began to plot against him.

"Let's kill him," said one.

"No," said Reuben. "We'll just put him down that dried-up well for a while. That'll teach him a lesson!"

So they grabbed Joseph and dragged him to the well.

"Let me go!" shouted Joseph, kicking and struggling to get free. "Watch out for my coat, you'll tear it!"

Joseph's brothers didn't care. They took the coat right off, then threw Joseph into the well. It was a deep pit. There was no escape. After that, as if nothing had happened, they sat down and had lunch. All except Reuben, who had gone to look for a stray lamb.

They had just finished eating, when along came some merchants on their way to Egypt. Judah had an idea. It wasn't a very nice one.

"Let's sell Joseph to the merchants," he said.

In those days people could be bought and sold in a slave market. The brothers could get rid of Joseph and earn some money too.

So while Reuben was still away, the others lifted Joseph out of the pit and sold him. They were paid twenty silver pieces, which was a good price.

By the time Reuben got back, Joseph was gone. At first Reuben thought the others had killed him. Then Daniel told him what they had done. Reuben was horrified to hear that Joseph had been taken to Egypt as a slave. But it was too late to do anything about it. What *would* they tell Jacob?

Judah, who was full of mean ideas, had a plan.

"We'll put some goat's blood on Joseph's coat," he said. "Father will think he was killed by a wild animal."

It was a cruel thing to do, but Jacob was sure to believe it. When the brothers returned home, you can imagine how upset Jacob was to see the bloodstained coat: Joseph's coat of many colors.

Tears fell from Jacob's eyes. The old man said he would be sad for the rest of his life.

Little did Jacob know that he *would* see his son again. For Joseph, the dreamer, became one of the most important people in Egypt. It happened like this:

During his time as a slave, Joseph was put into prison for something he hadn't done. While he was there, he told the other prisoners the meaning of their dreams. And he was always right!

Word soon got around, and one day the king of Egypt heard about Joseph. He asked him to explain the meaning of some strange dreams he was having.

The king was so pleased with Joseph that he set him free and made him governor of Egypt. Joseph did his job well, and made sure there was always enough food for people to eat.

Many years later Joseph's brothers came to Egypt to buy corn. The crops in their own country had dried up. Their families at home were starving. They had to go down on their knees and beg the governor of Egypt for food! So you see, Joseph's dream about his brothers bowing down before him came true.

At first the brothers did not recognize Joseph. But then he told them who he was. Joseph forgave his brothers for treating him so badly all those years ago. He sent them home with sacks full of corn, food, and money.

When the brothers returned home, Jacob could hardly believe the news about Joseph. His favorite son was alive!

So Jacob took his family to Egypt and saw Joseph again, and they all lived there happily for many years.

Moses

in the Bulrushes

The king of Egypt was worried. People from Israel had been living in his country for many years and having lots of children. If things went on like this, soon there would be more of them than Egyptians. Something had to be done.

So the king made a new law. Every Israelite baby boy was to be drowned in the River Nile. It was a terrible law, but the Israelites had to obey.

One day a baby boy was born to a mother called Jochebed. She and her husband already had a fine son and a daughter called Miriam.

Jochebed loved her new baby and couldn't bear to see him taken away. For three whole months she kept him hidden. It was difficult. Babies grow and babies cry. There came a day when Jochebed had to think of a better way to hide him from the Egyptian king's men.

Jochebed had often stood on the banks of the River Nile and watched the fishermen in their reed boats. The boats were woven from the tough bulrushes that grew by the river. It gave her an idea.

Jochebed took a basket made of reeds and covered it with tar to make it watertight. Miriam watched her mother as she worked. The basket made a perfect floating cradle just big enough to hold her baby brother!

Miriam helped her mother wrap the baby to keep him warm. She cried as Jochebed gently laid him in the basket. Miriam loved her brother.

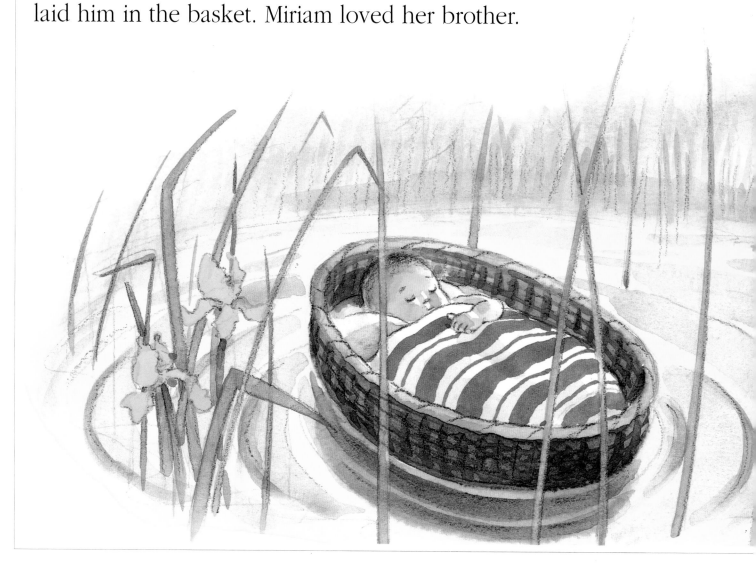

"It's for the best," said Jochebed, trying to comfort her. "We will hide him in the bulrushes. He will be safe there and you can keep watch over him."

Later, when they were sure no one was around, Miriam and her mother took the basket and hid it among the bulrushes. Then Jochebed went home, leaving Miriam to see what would happen.

Miriam was standing just near enough to the bulrushes to see the baby's cradle. Suddenly she heard a voice cry out. The king's daughter had come down to the river to bathe. She had found the baby!

"What's that basket over there?" said the princess to one of her maids. "Bring it to me."

The maid waded into the water and lifted the cradle out of the bulrushes. The baby was sound asleep, but as the princess took him into her arms, he woke up and began to cry. She loved him at once.

"Poor thing, it must be one of the Israelite babies," said the princess.

At that moment Miriam stepped from her hiding place and spoke to the king's daughter.

"Would you like me to find an Israelite woman to feed and look after the baby for you?" she asked.

The princess was delighted. Miriam knew just the right person for the job. She ran all the way home and got her mother!

So Jochebed was able to care for her son after all. The princess paid Jochebed to nurse the baby until he was old enough to go and live with her in the palace. Then she adopted the boy as her own son and called him Moses.

Moses grew up to be a very wise man, and God chose him to lead his people out of Egypt to a country of their own.

David
and Goliath

Along time ago there was a boy called David. His job was to look after the sheep on his father's farm. He was very good at it.

Each day David took the flock up the mountain to graze. He had to watch it carefully because there were hungry lions and bears around. They were always on the lookout for a stray sheep. But young David wasn't afraid. Not at all. He was one of the bravest shepherds around.

When a lion did manage to snatch a lamb from the flock, David ran after it. Even though he was unarmed, he chased the beast, sprang at it, and attacked it. It was so surprised that it immediately dropped the lamb. David wasn't afraid when the beast turned around to attack him. He fought and killed it. That's how brave he was!

When David wasn't busy with the sheep, he taught himself to play the harp. He was good at that too. One day King Saul heard about David and his music, and he asked the shepherd boy to play for him at the palace. So from that day on, the king often listened to David playing his harp.

Now, King Saul and the people of Israel were having trouble with their old enemies, the Philistines. They were always quarreling.

David's three oldest brothers were soldiers in King Saul's army. They had marched with the king to a mountain overlooking a valley. The Philistines were on the other side. The two armies stood facing each other, ready to do battle. Only this time things were different.

The Philistines had a soldier called Goliath, who was a real giant of a man. He was enormous! He wore a suit of heavy armor and had a shield as big as a door. To make matters worse, Goliath kept strutting up and down in front of King Saul's army, shouting at the top of his voice.

"Who's brave enough to fight me, eh?" bellowed Goliath. "Who's going to kill me?" he laughed. "Strike me dead, and we will be your slaves. But if I win . . . ha! Victory will be ours, and you will be *our* slaves!"

He went on and on like that for weeks. It was terrifying. Nobody dared go near him.

At home David wondered how his brothers were.

He wished he could fight, but he had to stay at home and look after the flocks.

One evening his father said, "I want you to take some food to your brothers and see how they are."

So early the next morning David set off for the mountain. It was a good long walk, and when he got there, the battle was about to begin. The armies were taking their positions. David found his brothers and they pointed to Goliath. "The king has promised that whoever kills Goliath will be rewarded with riches and shall marry his daughter," said one. "But there is no one brave enough to challenge him."

"Oh, yes, there is," said David. And he went straight to the king. "I'll fight Goliath for you."

At first the king refused. "You're just a boy," he said.

"I have killed lions and bears to save my father's sheep," said David. "God protected me then and he will save me from the giant."

The king wasn't too happy about it, but he agreed to let David try. He looked at David dressed in his thin tunic. "You must wear my armor," he said.

David tried it on, but everything was much too big. He couldn't move a step. So he took it all off, thanked the king, and said he would fight in his own way.

At a nearby stream, David chose five smooth, round stones and put them in a bag. Then he picked up his sling and went to meet Goliath.

The giant could hardly believe his eyes when he saw David. He had waited forty days for the king to choose somebody to fight him, and now he was sending a boy! Goliath roared with laughter. The sound was deafening, but David wasn't afraid.

The shepherd boy faced his enemy as Goliath came blundering forward.

"Come on," jeered Goliath. "I'm going to enjoy feeding you to the birds."

"You have come out to fight with a sword and a spear," said David boldly. "I have come in the name of God."

As Goliath moved toward him, David reached into his bag, took out a stone, and put it in his sling. He whirled it around so fast,

you couldn't see it spinning. Then he took aim and let the stone fly.

His aim was good. The stone smashed into the middle of the giant's forehead. With a dreadful cry Goliath crashed to the ground and lay there, dead. The Philistines gasped.

Quick as a blink, David grabbed Goliath's sword
and cut off the giant's head.

The Philistines were dumbfounded. Their
champion fighter was dead. The shepherd
boy had won the day. King Saul and his
army cheered and cheered. They
charged down the mountainside and
chased the Philistines out of sight.

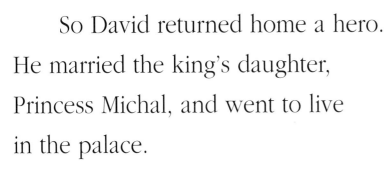

So David returned home a hero.
He married the king's daughter,
Princess Michal, and went to live
in the palace.

And much, much later, when
the old king died, David became
king of Israel.

Daniel

in the Lions' Den

King Darius was the king of Persia. He had more than a hundred officials to help him rule the land. His favorite was Daniel. Daniel was honest, wise, and loyal—and he never made mistakes. All the other men were jealous.

"King Darius never listens to us," they complained. "Daniel will be in charge of the country one day, you'll see."

It was true. King Darius had considered giving Daniel control of the whole empire. Daniel's enemies wanted to get rid of him. But how? Daniel never did anything wrong. He wouldn't lose his job that way. They had to think of something else.

Now, Daniel was a religious man. He worked hard for the king, but he was never too busy to pray to God. He prayed three times a day in his room in the palace. The other officials knew that and it gave them an idea.

One morning they went to see the king.

"We think there should be a new law," began one.

"To make your subjects obey you," said another.

They had written the law on a scroll for the king to sign. It said that people were forbidden to ask help from any god or man, except the king, for thirty days. If anyone disobeyed, they would be thrown to the lions! The king read it carefully.

"So if you will just sign here," said one of the officials rather hurriedly, "we will see that everyone obeys it."

King Darius signed the new law. He didn't suspect a thing. How could he have guessed that it was a wicked plot to kill Daniel?

After Daniel found out that the law was signed, he went to his room to pray as usual. He kneeled by his open window and gave thanks to God. His enemies spied on him as he prayed.

"Caught in the act!" they cried. And they marched right off to the king to tell him that Daniel prayed three times a day.

The king was very upset, but everyone, including Daniel, had to obey the law of the land. There was nothing King Darius could do to rescue him.

So that evening the king asked the palace guards to take Daniel down to the lions' den and throw him in. King Darius followed the men down to the den and spoke quietly to Daniel.

"I wish I could save you," he said. "Ask your god to protect you from the lions and keep you safe." Then the guards pushed Daniel into the den and rolled a big stone across the entrance.

The king walked back to the palace very sad. He was sure he would never see Daniel again.

Daniel slid down
into the den, his heart
thudding. He could smell
the lions at the bottom of
the pit. And they could
most certainly smell him!

Two lions padded out of
a cave and looked at Daniel
sprawled on the floor. They were
followed by two more. The poor beasts were thin and hungry.

Daniel crouched there, terrified, as the lions prowled around him and growled. He shut his eyes tight and prayed.

"Please, God, save me," he whispered. He had always trusted God to answer his prayers. No one else could help him now.

After a few minutes Daniel sat up slowly and opened his eyes. The lions opened their jaws . . .

and yawned. Daniel could see their long pink tongues and sharp teeth. The lions didn't seem to be hungry anymore. One came and rubbed its face against his leg. Another licked his hand. Then they all settled themselves comfortably around Daniel and began to purr. And before long those wild, ferocious beasts had curled up like kittens and were fast asleep.

Early the next morning King Darius ran to the den. He had spent all night worrying about Daniel in this dreadful place. Had Daniel's God saved him?

As the guards rolled the stone away, the king feared the worst. But he called out, "Daniel! Daniel!"

When Daniel shouted back, the king was astonished. The guards pulled Daniel out of the den. The king was amazed to see that there wasn't a scratch on him! King Darius hugged him happily and took him back to the palace.

The king told everyone how God had protected Daniel. He sent messengers all over the world to tell people to worship Daniel's God in the future.

As for all the scheming officials . . . they and their families were thrown into the lions' den and were never seen again!

Jonah

and the Whale

Now here's a strange tale about a man
called Jonah.

There was once a city called
Nineveh. It was a beautiful city, but
the people who lived there were
bad. Most of them were cruel and
wicked. God knew all about the
people of Nineveh. He wanted them
to change their ways. So one day God
spoke to Jonah.

"Go to Nineveh," he said, "and tell the people that if they don't stop being wicked, I will destroy them."

Jonah didn't think much of the idea. He knew how loving, patient, and understanding God was. God would rather forgive people than punish them.

"Forget that!" said Jonah to himself. "If the people of Nineveh are so wicked, they deserve to be punished. And if they change their ways, God will forgive them. Then I will have gone to all that trouble for nothing!"

So Jonah ran away. He packed a bag and hurried down to the harbor. He found a ship sailing that day. It was going on a long voyage. God will never find me so far away! thought Jonah as he paid his fare to the captain and went on board.

Jonah made himself comfortable below deck and settled down for a nap. The sea was calm as they sailed out of the harbor. But soon a terrible storm blew up. The wind howled. Huge waves crashed over the sides of the boat.

"All hands on deck!" bellowed the captain. "Throw the cargo overboard." That made the boat lighter and easier to steer. But the sailors were up to their knees in water. They were afraid and prayed to their gods. The captain went below to find Jonah, who was still asleep.

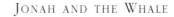

"Wake up!" shouted the captain. "We're in trouble. If the storm goes on like this, we'll all be drowned. Start praying to your god for help."

Jonah climbed on deck, where the crew was trying to find out who had caused the storm. They all wrote their names down and put them in a hat. The captain picked one out. It was Jonah's!

"Tell us! Who's to blame? And who are you anyway?" they cried.

Jonah had some explaining to do. He knew the storm was all his fault. He told the sailors that he worshipped God. God had seen him running away and was angry with him.

"Quick!" he said. "Throw me overboard. The storm will stop when I have gone."

So the sailors prayed that God would understand, and they threw Jonah out of the boat. And as soon as he splashed into the water, the wind dropped and the sea was as calm as a fish pond.

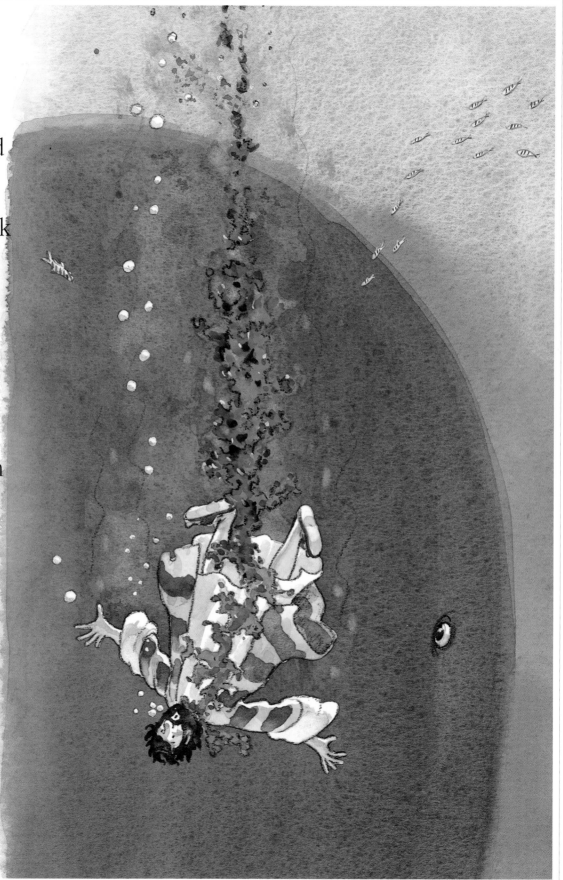

Down, down,
down. Jonah
sank like a
stone. Seaweed
wrapped itself
around his neck
and water
bubbled in his
mouth. It was
dark and silent
beneath the
waves as Jonah
sank deeper
and deeper
until . . .
Bump!
Jonah's head
touched
something
slippery and
soft.

He was about to grab it, when he found himself spinning around in a whirlpool. Jonah flapped his arms and spluttered. He was swept along a passageway, like a spider swirling down a drain. And just when it seemed he would never stop tumbling head over heels, he landed in a sort of cave.

He had been swallowed by a whale!

Jonah sat up and looked around. It was damp and sticky and smelled of rotting seaweed. Jonah cried. God would never find him now. He spent three long days and nights inside the whale. Then he thanked God for keeping him alive under the sea and asked for forgiveness. Jonah promised to go to Nineveh if he got out alive.

God knew Jonah was sorry. He forgave Jonah and told the whale to let him out on the nearest beach. Then the whale swam close to the shore, opened its enormous mouth, and spat Jonah out onto the sand. He was shaking with cold and hunger.

For a while Jonah lay in the sunshine and took deep breaths of fresh air. It was good to be out of that smelly whale. When Jonah had recovered, God spoke to him and told him to go to Nineveh.

"Tell the people to change their wicked ways or I will punish them," he said.

This time Jonah went to Nineveh at once. The people of that beautiful city listened to him. They were sorry for behaving so badly and began to change for the better.

God was very pleased. He forgave them for being so wicked and didn't punish them at all. Jonah was furious about it. He thought the people of Nineveh should have been punished.

"I knew this would happen!" he shouted. "I've come all this way for nothing."

God spoke quietly to Jonah. "Don't be angry," he said. "I forgave them because they were sorry."

Jonah thought for a moment and said, "Just as you forgave me inside the whale?"

"Yes," said God. "It's best to forgive."

And Jonah had to agree that he was right.

The First Christmas

The Great Augustus, emperor of
Rome, was counting people. In
Palestine, which was part of the Roman
empire, everyone had to pay taxes—
sums of money that helped to pay for
the army or for building towns and
roads. The emperor was working out
how much he could expect to be paid,
by adding up the number of people
living there. It was quite a business.

Everybody had to record their names in the place where they were born. Those who had moved away had to go all the way back to be counted. The roads were full of men and women walking from one place to another.

A carpenter called Joseph and his wife, Mary, were doing just that. They had come from Nazareth, along the River Jordan to Bethlehem. It was a long journey.

Mary was riding a donkey. It was not a good time for her to travel. She was expecting a baby. A very special baby. An angel had told Mary she was to be the mother of God's son, the most blessed baby ever born. And here she was, riding a donkey!

Bethlehem was crowded when they arrived. Mary and Joseph were tired and hungry after their long journey. So was the donkey. They went straight to the inn to rest.

"I'm sorry," said the innkeeper, "there's no room. I've been full with visitors for days."

No room! Joseph was really worried. They had to stay somewhere. Mary's baby was due at any moment.

By late evening the best they could find was a stable. The owner could see they were desperate. He moved his animals into one stall, and gave Mary and Joseph the other.

Mary made herself as comfortable as she could on a bed of straw, while the donkey munched hay from a manger. Joseph lit an oil lamp and watched anxiously over his wife.

And later, in the glow of lamplight, Mary's special baby was born. She called him Jesus, as the angel had told her to do.

Now, there were shepherds in the hills around Bethlehem that night, looking after their sheep. It was a cold, clear night. The shepherds wrapped their cloaks around themselves and kept a sharp lookout for wild animals.

All was dark and quiet and still.

Suddenly they were surrounded by a brilliant light. It was as if the sun and moon were shining together on the very spot where they were sitting. It frightened the shepherds, I can tell you. They had never known anything like it. Then a voice spoke out of the brightness. It was an angel.

"Don't be afraid," said the angel. "I have good news for you. A king has been born in Bethlehem. The baby is your Savior, Christ the Lord. Go and see him for yourselves."

The shepherds could hardly believe their ears. They stared at each other in wonder.

"You will find the baby wrapped warmly and lying in a manger," said the angel, who knew that they were astonished.

As soon as the angel had spoken, the shepherds heard voices singing praises to God. The whole sky seemed to be singing! Then the light dimmed and the voices faded into the night. The shepherds stared up at the stars, but the angel had gone. And all was quiet again.

"We must go to Bethlehem at once," said the shepherds, remembering what the angel had told them. So they left their sheep and hurried over the fields to look for the newborn king.

When the shepherds got to the stable, they found Mary and Joseph and saw the baby Jesus lying in a manger. It was just as the angel had said. He was wrapped in cloths and looked snug in his cradle of hay. The Son of God had been born in a stable!

The shepherds were not the only ones to hear about the baby. Three wise men, living far away in another country, had been told about the new king too. They traveled all the way to Bethlehem on camels, following a big, bright star. The star took them right to the place where Jesus lay.

Mary and Joseph welcomed the travelers as they came to worship the royal child. The wise men brought the baby precious gifts of gold, frankincense, and myrrh—gifts fit for a king—that very first Christmas, nearly two thousand years ago.

The Good Samaritan

When Jesus grew up, he spent his time teaching people about God and being kind to one another. He was always being asked questions. Sometimes Jesus answered with a story, and asked his listeners to work out the answer for themselves. Which is how this story came about.

A clever teacher of the law once said to Jesus, "What do I have to do to live forever? The law says we should love God with all our hearts and love our neighbors as much as ourselves. But who is my neighbor?" The teacher was testing Jesus. He hoped to hear that he should love only his friends. So Jesus told him a story about a traveler.

A man was walking from Jerusalem to Jericho. It was a long walk and the road passed through lonely, hilly country. It was a dangerous road. Robbers and bandits hid among the rocks.

Sure enough, as the traveler walked along, a gang of robbers sprang from a hiding place. They knocked the man to the ground, beat him, and stole his money and clothes. Then the gang ran off, leaving him lying in the road.

After a while a priest came along. The very person to help someone in trouble, you might think. But he didn't. He took one look at the injured man and hurried by on the other side of the road. He was afraid the robbers might attack him too.

Shortly afterward another man came along. He worked in the temple. But he didn't stop either. He took a closer look at the man, then like the priest, hurried by on the other side.

The sun beat down and the flies buzzed around the man's wounds. It seemed as if the poor traveler was to be left to die on that desolate country road.

Much later the sound of a donkey's hooves could be heard in the distance. It was a man on his way to Jericho. He was a Samaritan.

Now, the man who had been injured was a Jew, and the Jews and the Samaritans were old enemies. The Jews thought of the Samaritans as foreigners and wouldn't speak to them. So it was unlikely the Samaritan would stop to help.

But as soon as the Samaritan saw the injured man, he got off his donkey and went to him. He took wine from his saddlebag and cleaned the man's wounds. Then he bathed the wounds with soothing oil and bandaged them. After that the Samaritan gently lifted the man onto his donkey and took him to the nearest inn.

He stayed with the man that night to make sure he was comfortable.

In the morning the Samaritan had to be on his way again. Before he left, he paid the innkeeper two silver coins to look after the man until he was better. He promised to pay the innkeeper on his way back for anything more.

When Jesus had finished telling this story, he turned to the clever teacher and said, "Which of the three men do you think loved the injured man like a neighbor?"

The clever teacher didn't feel quite so clever now.

"The Samaritan," he admitted. "The one who was kind to him."

"You're right," said Jesus. "Now go, and be like him."

Jesus

Heals Jairus's Daughter

There was once a man called Jairus, who lived with his wife in a town called Capernaum. The couple had a daughter, and they loved her more than anything.

Now, when their daughter was twelve years old, she became ill. The best doctor in town was sent for, but as the days went by, the little girl grew worse. Jairus and his wife spent hours at her bedside, trying to comfort her.

One morning as Jairus sat bathing his daughter with cool water, he heard voices down by the shore. Capernaum was by Lake Galilee, and the beach was a short walk from the house.

"What's going on?" said Jairus to a servant. He was afraid the noise would disturb the sick child.

"Jesus of Nazareth arrived by boat this morning," said the servant. "He came with twelve friends."

Jairus had heard so much about Jesus. He had been told that Jesus had the power to heal people. And here he was, in Capernaum! If anyone could help his daughter, it was Jesus.

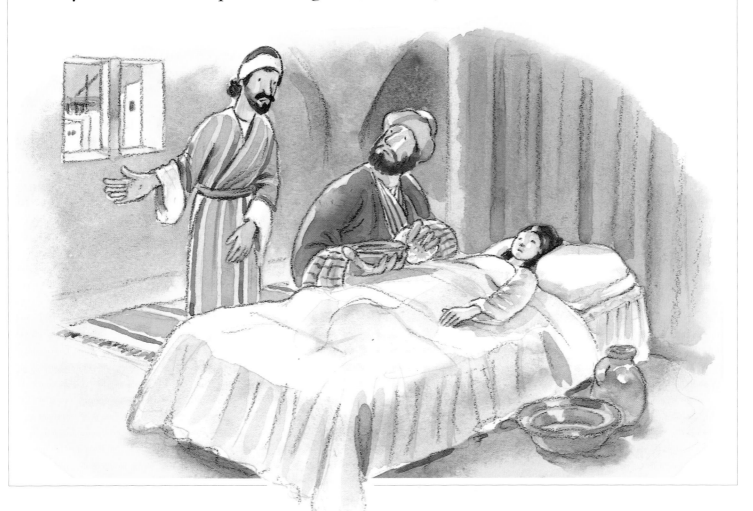

Without a word, Jairus left the house and ran outside. He hurried through the streets and down to the shore. Quite a crowd had gathered around Jesus. But when they saw Jairus rushing toward them, they made way. Jairus was an important man in the town, and many people knew him.

"Jairus looks upset," said one.

"I wonder what he wants with Jesus?" said another.

Jairus ran up to Jesus and fell at his feet.

"Master," he said, "please come quickly. My daughter is very ill. Only you can make her well. If you don't come, she will die!"

Of course Jesus said he would help. He could see that Jairus trusted him completely— that was very important. But on the way there something happened. There was a crowd following Jesus, bumping and jostling each other to stay close. Suddenly Jesus stopped and asked, "Who touched me?"

Well, I ask you, what a question! There were so many pushing and shoving. Everyone was quiet. So Jesus asked again.

"Who touched me?"

As Jesus looked around, a frightened woman stepped forward.

"I touched you," said the woman nervously. "I have been ill for many years and have spent all my money on doctors. I knew if I could only touch the hem of your cloak, I would be cured."

So that was it! In all the hustle and bustle, at the very moment the woman had touched his cloak, Jesus had felt some healing power flow out of him.

Jesus looked at the woman with such kindness. "Your trust in me has cured you," he said gently.

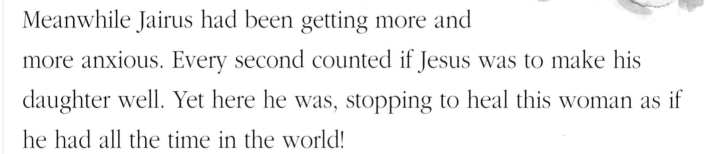

Meanwhile Jairus had been getting more and more anxious. Every second counted if Jesus was to make his daughter well. Yet here he was, stopping to heal this woman as if he had all the time in the world!

Jairus was about to plead with Jesus to hurry up, when he saw his servant coming to meet him. He had sad news.

"Your daughter is dead," he said. "There is no need to trouble Jesus anymore."

Jairus wept. His daughter had just died, and the only man who could have saved her was so near. But Jesus simply turned to Jairus and said, "Go on trusting me."

Then he took three of his friends, Peter, James, and John, and went to see the child. Jairus and his wife cried as Jesus sat down at her bedside.

"She is only sleeping," Jesus said as he took her small, cold hand in his. "Get up, my child," he said quietly.

The little girl's eyes flickered open. As she felt her strength returning, she sat up, smiled at Jesus . . . and jumped out of bed!

You can imagine how thankful those parents were to see their daughter alive and well again.

Jesus smiled at them. He loved children and it made him happy too.

"And now," he said, "it's time to prepare some food. I think you'll find your daughter is hungry!"

The Story of the Loaves and Fishes

No one knows the name of the little boy in this story, so I shall call him Thomas.

Thomas lived in a tiny village tucked away in the hills overlooking Lake Galilee. It was a lonely life and he was often bored. He had no brothers or sisters to play with that I know of—only a few goats. And they weren't much fun.

One day Thomas decided to go for a walk down by the lake. He liked climbing rocks and looking for crabs in the sand.

"Take some food," said his mother, "and be careful."

She packed a bag with five barley loaves and two small fishes, and Thomas set off. He was scrambling down a bank when he saw a strange sight.

Thomas squinted his eyes, and to his surprise he saw a great many people walking along the shore. They were coming toward him. Usually he would be lucky to find one person to talk to. But today he'd have hundreds! Maybe even some children his own age!

Then Thomas looked down on the lake and saw a boat full of men approaching. Jesus was sitting in the middle.

Jesus saw Thomas climbing down to the shore. He
and his friends had come here for a quiet day in the
hills. They had all been busy preaching in the cities
around Galilee and needed some time alone.

But the crowd was following Jesus. Many of them had seen
him heal people, and they were amazed by his incredible power.

While Jesus and his friends found a spot in the hills, Thomas watched the people approaching. He was sure there were more than a few hundred. It looked like thousands! Thomas was beginning to feel hungry. Probably all these people were too. He was glad his mother had packed him a lunch.

Jesus also saw the crowd coming and had pity on them. They had followed him all this way and had brought nothing with them to eat.

"Where can we buy enough food to feed all these people?" Jesus asked his friend Philip. He already knew the answer, but Philip didn't know that.

"It would cost a fortune," replied Philip. "Two hundred silver coins wouldn't buy enough bread for each to have even a little piece."

Andrew, another of Jesus's friends, had seen Thomas's lunch bag.

"Look," said Andrew, "that boy has some food."

"Come," said Jesus to Thomas, who was sitting nearby. "Let me see what you have."

Thomas was hungry, but he gave his food to Jesus.

Philip laughed. "There are only five barley loaves and two small fishes. Hardly enough to go around this crowd!"

Jesus knew differently.

"Tell the people to sit down," he told Philip and Andrew as he took the food. While they were seating the crowd in small groups, Jesus gave thanks to God and began to break the food into small pieces.

Jesus's friends helped him by giving out handfuls of bread and fish to everyone there. Handfuls and handfuls! Enough to feed all those people until they were full. Thomas was astonished. Jesus had fed over five thousand people from the five barley loaves and two small fishes.

At the end of the meal Jesus told his friends to pick up any food that was left over. He didn't want to waste anything. And do you know, they collected twelve baskets full of scraps!

That evening Thomas ran home to tell his mother all that had happened. It was a day he would remember for the rest of his life.